O N

CW00959051

THOMAS MERTON ON EASTERN MEDITATION

Edited, with an introduction, by Bonnie Thurston

A NEW DIRECTIONS BOOK

Acknowledgments and permissions can be found on page 76.

NOTE: While the editor marked all passages scrupulously, some ellipses
and other editorial indications have been omitted by the publisher to
present a smoother text to the general reader.

Manufactured in the United States of America
New Directions Books are printed on acid-free paper.
First published as a New Directions Paperbook (NDP1227) in 2012
Design by Erik Rieselbach

Library of Congress Cataloging-in-Publication Data
Merton, Thomas, 1915–1968.
[Selections. 2012]
On Eastern meditation / Thomas Merton ; edited, with an
introduction, by Bonnie Thurston.
p. cm. — (New Directions paperbook ; NDP 1226)
ISBN 978-0-8112-1994-5 (alk. paper) — ISBN 978-0-8112-1995-2
1. Christianity and other religions—Asian. 2. Asia—Religion.
3. Meditation—Asia. 4. Spiritual life—Comparative studies.
5. East and West. I. Thurston, Bonnie. II. Title.
BR128.A77M46 2012
261.2'4—dc23

2012001973

10 9 8 7 6 5 4 3 2 1

New Directions Books are published for James Laughlin
by New Directions Publishing Corporation
80 Eighth Avenue, New York, New York 10011

ndbooks.com

In gratitude for my extended "Thomas Merton family," and the International Thomas Merton Society, its Chapters and Affiliates, especially the Thomas Merton Society of Great Britain and Ireland.

CONTENTS

ON MERTON AND THE EAST
AN INTRODUCTION

On September 9, 1968, days before he left his Kentucky monastery for the Asian pilgrimage on which he died, the Trappist monk Thomas Merton (1915–1968), copied the following from Robinson Jeffers's poem "The Torch-Bearers' Race" into his journal:

> We have climbed at length to a height, to an end, this end:
> shall we go down again to Mother Asia?
> Some of us will go down, some will abide....[1]

How much did this convert to Roman Catholicism know about "Mother Asia"? Why was he so anxious to visit her? These questions are appropriately raised by someone reading a collection of Merton's thoughts on Eastern meditation. This brief introduction hopes to answer these questions and to explain the book's principles of organization and selection.

Merton's journey to "Mother Asia," "... a physical fact

---

1. *The Other Side of the Mountain: The Journals of Thomas Merton* (Volume 7, 1967–1968) Patrick Hart, O.C.S.O., editor (San Francisco: HarperSanFrancisco, 1999), 167.

and a psychological and spiritual actualization of a symbolic movement,"[2] began long before 1968. As a student at Oakham School in England in the late 1920s, he argued the pro-Gandhi side in a debate (and lost). At Columbia University in the 1930s he read Huxley's *Ends and Means* and Father Wieger's French translations of Oriental texts, and he met a Hindu monk, Bramachari, who encouraged him to read Christian classics. Some scholars think this led to Merton's conversion to Christianity. By then a professed monk at Gethsemani, Merton in his 1949 journal (published as *The Sign of Jonas*) mentions a postulant who received Zen training, as well as correspondence with an Indian in Simla about Pantajali's yoga. Br. Patrick Hart, one of Merton's novices, reports that in the 1960s D. T. Suzuki stimulated Merton's interest in Zen. By the late 1960s Merton had studied in the best English translations then available not only Zen, but also Raja Yoga, Tibetan Buddhism, Theravada Buddhism, Madhyamika philosophy, Hinduism, Shankara's Avaita Vedanta, the Bhagavad Gita, Confucianism, and Taoism (particularly Chuang Tzu). He had also practiced calligraphy and brush painting.

Merton was convinced there was a "real possibility of contact on a deep level between ... contemplative and monastic tradition in the West and the various contemplative traditions in the East...."[3] He wrote in *Conjectures*

2. Deba P. Patnaik, "Syllables of a Great Song: Merton and Asian Religious Thought" in *The Message of Thomas Merton*, ed. Patrick Hart, O.C.S.O. (Kalamazoo, MI: Cistercian Publications, 1981), 75.

3. *The Asian Journal of Thomas Merton* (New York: New Directions, 1973), 311.

of a Guilty Bystander, "If I affirm myself as a Catholic merely by denying all that is Muslim, Jewish, Protestant, Hindu, Buddhist, etc., in the end I will find that there is not much left for me to affirm as a Catholic: and certainly no breath of the Spirit with which to affirm it."[4] Merton's study of Asian religions led to several publications. After his paraphrase of the Taoist text *The Way of Chuang Tzu* (1965) and his collection of sayings of Gandhi, *Gandhi on Non-Violence* (1965), Merton's largest body of writing on Eastern religions is on Zen. It includes *Mystics and Zen Masters* (1967), *Zen and the Birds of Appetite* (1968), the posthumously published *Asian Journal of Thomas Merton* (1973), and *Introductions East and West* (1981), as well as letters to a dizzying and dazzling array of Eastern scholars and practitioners including Masao Abe, Amiya Chakravarty, Heinrich Dumoulin, Thích Nhất Hạnh, William Johnson, Marco Pallis, John C. H. Wu, and several Tibetan lamas, including H. H. the Dalai Lama.

Merton "went East," not as a tourist, but as a monastic pilgrim. He noted in a talk planned for Calcutta in October 1968, "I come as a pilgrim ... to drink from ancient sources of monastic vision and experience. I seek ... to become a better and more enlightened monk.... [W]e have now reached a stage of (long-overdue) religious maturity at which it may be possible for someone to remain perfectly faithful to a Christian and Western monastic commitment, and ... to learn in depth from ... a

4. Thomas Merton, *Conjectures of a Guilty Bystander* (New York: Doubleday/Image, 1966/68), 144.

Buddhist or Hindu discipline and experience."[5] On July 9, 1968, he wrote to Dom Willibrord Van Dikj, "I am particularly interested, when in the Orient, in making some contacts with non-Christian monks, above all Buddhists, as I am quite involved in the study of comparative mysticism — or ways of 'contemplation' — and in relations with Buddhists and Hindus."[6] The pilgrim monk sought spiritual support for his journey, imploring Dom Jacques Winandy, "Pray for me. I am going to India. I believe this is one of the greatest graces of my life and I look forward to meeting many monks of other traditions, particularly Buddhists. The experience could be invaluable. But it will need much prayer."[7]

When Merton turned toward "Mother Asia," he was not rejecting his religious tradition and commitment, not leaving something behind, but enlarging his (already expansive) heart's embrace. Merton looked East for language to articulate his Christian, monastic, spiritual experience, for a cultural alternative to what he saw as the corruptions of Western society,[8] to explore techniques to

5. *The Asian Journal of Thomas Merton.* 312–13. (For a fuller discussion see also pp. 337–44.) Merton reiterated this monastic focus in letters to Amiya Chakravarty; M. Myriam Dardenne, O.C.S.O.; Finley Peter Dunne, Jr.; and Dom Jacques Winandy. A retrospective analysis ten years after Merton's death, "Merton and the East" by Jean Leclercq, O.S.B. (*Cistercian Studies Quarterly*, 8/4, 1978) confirmed Merton's "purpose remained essentially monastic, directed towards interior growth and not to the acquisition of knowledge. . . ." (312)

6. *The School of Charity: The Letters of Thomas Merton on Religious Renewal and Spiritual Direction*, ed. Patrick Hart, O.C.S.O., (New York: Harcourt Brace Jovanovich, 1990), 388.

7. Ibid. 403–4.

8 Merton wrote to Amiya Chakravarty: "More and more I feel that Asia

facilitate his own spiritual growth, and to encourage the monastic renewal initiated by the Second Vatican Council. In her outstanding selection of Merton's writings, Christine Bochen makes the point incisively:

> Neither a professional ecumenist nor a specialist in inter-religious Dialogue, Merton modeled a way of encounter and dialogue.... Deeply rooted in his own tradition, he was open and receptive to the wisdom of the world's religions. Merton embodied the spirit that is essential to building unity: he was open to the experience and perspective of others and respectful of their beliefs and practice. He was also clear and firm in his own faith convictions. Searching for common ground, he knew well, does not mean discounting one's own roots.[9]

In his "Letter to Pablo Antonio Cuadra Concerning Giants," which appears in what may be his best collection of poetry, *Emblems of a Season of Fury* (1963), Merton tellingly writes, "It is my belief that we should not be too sure of having found Christ in ourselves until we have found him also in the part of humanity that is most remote from our own" and "God speaks, and God is to be heard, not only on Sinai, not only in my own heart, by in the *voice of the stranger*" (italics Merton's).[10]

is in so many ways more congenial to me than the West." *The Hidden Ground of Love: the Letters of Thomas Merton on Religious Experience and Social Concerns*, ed. William H. Shannon, (New York: Farrar, Straus and Giroux, 1985), 118.

9. Christine M. Bochen, ed., *Thomas Merton: Essential Writings* (Maryknoll, NY: Orbis Books, 2000), 140–41.

10. *The Collected Poems of Thomas Merton* (New York: New Directions, 1977), 382–83 and 384.

In "Thomas Merton in Dialogue with Eastern Religions," the Merton scholar William Shannon noted five insights from Western spiritual classics that resonate with what Merton found in the East: "(1) the priority of experience over speculation; (2) the inadequacy of words to articulate religious experience; (3) the fundamental oneness of all reality; (4) the realization that the goal of all spiritual discipline is transformation of consciousness; and (5) 'purity of heart'... liberation from attachment."[11] These themes are represented in this volume and in Merton's attitude in a 1963 letter to Marco Pallis: "... I have a deep affinity and respect for Buddhism, and I think that I am as much a Chinese Buddhist in temperament and spirit as I am a Christian.... I think one can certainly believe in the revealed truths of Christianity and follow Christ, while at the same time having a Buddhist outlook on life and nature.... A certain element of Buddhism in culture and spirituality is by no means incompatible with Christian belief...."[12]

Merton's pilgrimage East was not about what in *Gandhi on Non-Violence* he called "laughable syncretisms,"[13] not about "syncretism, indifferentism, the vapid and careless friendliness that accepts everything by thinking of nothing."[14] The most profound pilgrimages

11. William H. Shannon, "Thomas Merton in Dialogue with Eastern Religions," in *The Vision of Thomas Merton*, Patrick F. O'Connell, ed. (Notre Dame, IN: Ave Maria Press, 2003), 214.

12. *The Hidden Ground of Love*, 465.

13. Thomas Merton, *Gandhi on Non-Violence* (New York: New Directions, 1965/2007), 6.

14. *Conjectures of a Guilty Bystander*, 144.

are made by those with homes which they have voluntarily left and to which they can return. Although Merton believed religious dialogue "must take place under the true monastic conditions of quiet, tranquility, sobriety, leisureliness, reverence, meditation, and cloistered peace,"[15] his principles for "contemplative dialogue" are universally applicable: Dialogue is for

> those who have entered with full seriousness into their own ... tradition....
>
> Second, there can be no question of a facile syncretism. ...
>
> Third, there must be a scrupulous respect for important differences....
>
> Fourth, attention must be concentrated on ... the area of true self-transcendence and enlightenment....
>
> Fifth, questions of institutional structure, monastic rule, traditional forms of cult and observance must be seen as relatively secondary and are not to become the central focus of attention."[16]

These principles rest on a conviction articulated in *Zen and the Birds of Appetite*. "All religions ... 'meet at the top,' and their various theologies and philosophies become irrelevant when we see that they were merely means for arriving at the same end...."[17]

That religions "meet at the top" brings us to this sampling of Merton's thought on that universal journey to

---

15. *The Asian Journal*, 313.
16. *The Asian Journal*, 316–17.
17. Thomas Merton, *Zen and the Birds of Appetite* (New York: New Directions, 1968), 43.

"the top." I interpret "meditation" not narrowly as a religious practice, but broadly as a life stance, a world view founded in the practice of prayer. Meditation's contemplative stance is "grounded" in landscape, built on teaching, and reflects particular practices. This is reflected in the book's three divisions, which draw heavily from Merton's thoughts on Buddhism, the Eastern tradition with which he was most familiar. There are occasional references to Christianity because Merton was a Christian, and because by geographical origin Christianity *is* an Eastern (Asian) religion.

I admit to a certain dis-ease with "extracting nuggets" from their contexts. My defense is that Merton himself followed this practice in *The Wisdom of the Desert* (1960), *Gandhi on Non-Violence* (1965), and *The Way of Chuang Tzu* (1965), and in quotations in the journal he kept during his final journey. Merton notes his collection from Chuang Tzu is "the result of five years of reading, study, annotation, and meditation."[18] I have studied Merton since 1976.

Language has changed since the 1960s. A particular difficulty is that Merton's language is not gender-inclusive. This grates on the contemporary ear. I hope the dissonance will not obscure the truths spoken, because it seemed dishonest to change Merton's words. Explanatory "alterations" occur in brackets. Quotations are followed by a parenthesis giving their source. When a quotation is

18. Thomas Merton, *The Way of Chuang Tzu* (New York: New Directions, 1965), 9.

itself a quotation (Merton quoting Gandhi, for example) the reference includes Merton's citation. Apparatus is minimal to avoid distracting from the beauty of Merton's thought. A list of works cited, with abbreviations, precedes the text, and a brief glossary of unfamiliar terms appears at the end of the book. Definitions are drawn largely from those in Merton's *Asian Journal*.

I hope sampling these small, dense morsels might entice you to read the volumes from which they come. I hope they will assist and be good companions on your journey "to the top." Of *Zen and the Birds of Appetite* Merton said, "the purpose of this present book is not apologetic."[19] Nor is the purpose of *this* book, which echoes Merton's prayer for his friends in a circular letter of September 1968 as he left Gethsemani Abbey for "Mother Asia": "Our real journey in life is interior; it is a matter of growth, deepening, and of an ever greater surrender to the creative action of love and grace in our hearts. Never was it more necessary for us to respond to that action. I pray that we may all do so."[20]

—BONNIE THURSTON

19. *Zen and the Birds of Appetite*, 15.
20. *The Asian Journal*, 296.

ABBREVIATIONS

AJ   Naomi Burton (et al., eds.), *The Asian Journal of Thomas Merton* (New York: New Directions, 1968)

CP   *The Collected Poems of Thomas Merton* (New York: New Directions, 1977)

GNV Thomas Merton (ed.), *Gandhi On Non Violence* (New York: New Directions, 1965)

HGL William H. Shannon (ed.), *The Hidden Ground of Love* (Thomas Merton Letters) (New York: Farrar, Straus and Giroux, 1985)

IEW Robert E. Daggy (ed.), *Thomas Merton: Introductions East and West* (The Foreign Prefaces of Thomas Merton) (Greensboro: Unicorn Press, Inc., 1981)

MZM Thomas Merton, *Mystics and Zen Masters* (New York: Dell/Delta Books, 1965)

WCZ Thomas Merton, *The Way of Chuang Tzu* (New York: New Directions, 1965)

WF   William H. Shannon (ed.), *Witness to Freedom* (Thomas Merton Letters in Times of Crisis) (New York: Farrar, Straus and Giroux, 1994)

ZBA Thomas Merton, *Zen and the Birds of Appetite* (New York: New Directions, 1968)

I seek to speak to you, in some way, as your own self. Who can tell what this may mean? I myself do not know. But if you listen, things will be said that are perhaps not written in this book. And this will be due not to me, but to One who lives and speaks in both! (*IEW* 47)

ON LANDSCAPE

Last night I had a curious dream about Kanchenjunga. I was looking at the mountain and it was pure white, absolutely pure, especially the peaks that lie to the west. And I saw the pure beauty of their shape and outline, all in white. And I heard a voice saying—or got the clear idea of: "There is another side to the mountain." I realized that it was turned around and everything was lined up differently....

There is another side of Kanchenjunga and of every mountain—the side that has never been photographed and turned into post cards. That is the only side worth seeing.

(*AJ* 152–53)

Our real journey in life is interior: it is a matter of growth, deepening, and of an ever great surrender to the creative action of love and grace in our hearts. Never was it more necessary for us to respond to that action.

(*AJ* 296)

And the Buddha pointed to the earth and called it to witness that it did not belong to Mara, because he had just obtained enlightenment on it.

(*AJ* 341)

When great Nature sighs, we hear the winds
Which, noiseless in themselves,
Awaken voices from other beings,
Blowing on them.   (ii.I. *WCZ* 38)

No writing on the solitary, meditative dimensions of life
can say anything that has not already been said better by
the wind in the pine trees.   (*IEW* 91)

Polonnaruwa with its vast area under trees. Fences. Few
people. No beggars. A dirt road. Lost.... Distant mountains, like Yucatan.

The path dips down to Gal Vihara: a wide, quiet, hol-
low, surrounded with trees. A low outcrop of rock, with a
cave cut into it, and beside the cave a big seated Buddha
on the left, a reclining Buddha on the right, and Ananda,
I guess, standing by the head of the reclining Buddha. In
the cave, another seated Buddha....

Looking at these figures I was suddenly, almost forc-
ibly, jerked clean out of the habitual, half-tied vision of
things, and an inner clearness, clarity, as if exploding from
the rocks themselves, became evident and obvious.... All
problems are resolved and everything is clear, simply because what matters is clear. The rock, all matter, all life,
is charged with dharmakaya ... everything is emptiness
and everything is compassion. I don't know when in my
life I have ever had such a sense of beauty and spiritual
validity running together in one aesthetic illumination.
Surely, with Mahabalipuram and Polonnaruwa my Asian
pilgrimage has come clear and purified itself. I mean, I

know and have seen what I was obscurely looking for. I don't know what else remains but I have now seen and have pierced through the surface and have got beyond the shadow and the disguise. (*AJ* 233, 235–36)

I occasionally meet my own kind of Zen master, in passing, and for a brief moment. For example, the other day a bluebird sitting on a fence post suddenly took off after a wasp, dived for it, missed, and instantly returned to the same position on the fence post as if nothing had ever happened. A brief, split-second lesson in Zen . . . the birds never stop to say "I missed" because, in fact, whether they catch the wasp or not, they never miss. (*HGL* 563)

The geographical pilgrimage is the symbolic acting out of an inner journey. The inner journey is the interpolation of the meanings and signs of the outer pilgrimage. One can have one without the other. It is best to have both.

(*MZM* 92)

[Chuang Tzu's] respect for the wholeness of reality which cannot be seized in a definition. The real meaning of *nature*. One must respect nature before one can rise out of it to be a person. (*HGL* 614, italics Merton's)

ON TEACHING / *DHARMA*

DHARMA: GENERAL

Is there to be found on earth a fullness of joy, or is there no such thing? Is there some way to make life fully worth living, or is this impossible? If there is such a way, how do you go about finding it? What should you try to do? What should you seek to avoid? What should be the goal in which your activity comes to rest? What should you accept? What should you refuse to accept? What should you love?

(*WCZ* 99)

No road, no path,
No land marks
Show the way there.
You must go by the stars.

(*CP* 319)

It is most important first of all to understand deeply and live one's own tradition, not confusing it with what is foreign to it, if one is to seriously appreciate other traditions and distinguish in them what is close to one's own and what is, perhaps, irreconcilable with one's own. The great danger at the moment is a huge muddling and confusing of the spiritual traditions that still survive. (*WF* 313)

The Master said: "Where you do not understand, there is the point for your understanding." (*ZBA* 53)

Faith means doubt. Faith is not the suppression of doubt. It is the overcoming of doubt, and you overcome doubt by going through it. (*AJ* 306)

When the right moment arrives, even one who seems incapable of any instruction whatever will become mysteriously aware of Tao. (*WCZ* 31)

What is important is not liberation from the body but liberation from the mind. We are not entangled in our own body but entangled in our own mind. (*AJ* 90)

You never find happiness until you stop looking for it. (*WCZ* 101)

The pivot of Tao passes through the center where all affirmations and denials converge. He who grasps the pivot is at the still-point from which all movements and oppositions can be seen in their right relationship. (*WCZ* 43)

Great knowledge sees all in one.
Small knowledge breaks down into the many. (*WCZ* 40)

The whole meaning of the *Great Learning* is that right action depends on the awareness of the person acting.

(MZM 60, italics Merton's)

We can no longer rely on being supported by structures that may be destroyed at any moment.... You cannot rely on structures. The time for relying on structures has disappeared.

(AJ 338)

Don't read anything that robs you of sleep: sleep is better than reading.

(HGL 633)

Wisdom

I studied it and it taught me nothing.
I learned it and soon forgot everything else:
Having forgotten, I was burdened with knowledge—
The insupportable knowledge of nothing.

How sweet my life would be, if I were wise!
Wisdom is well known
When it is no longer seen or thought of.
Only then is understanding bearable.

(CP 279)

TEACHERS / *GURU*

"No one is so wrong as the man who knows all the answers."
                                                    (WCZ 27)

If I insist on giving you my truth, and never stop to receive your truth in return, then there can be no truth between us.
                                                    (CP 383)

In the cultivation of an inner spiritual consciousness there is a perpetual danger of self-deception, narcissism, self-righteous evasion of truth.... The hazard of the spiritual quest is ... that its genuineness cannot be left to our own isolated subjective judgment alone.   *(AJ 352)*

Nothing too clear was said about meditation, except that it has degrees and must be preceded by study. "Anyone" can do the simpler kind but a master is needed for the "more advanced."
                                                    (AJ 66)

[The Khempo of Namgyal, the Dalai Lama's private chaplain] stressed the need of a master for progress in meditation.... He insisted on the "ax of true doctrine" which must be used to cut the root of ignorance — and that one must know how to use the ax, otherwise he harms himself. So a man who is skilled in catching snakes can safely catch them but one who is not skilled gets bitten.

(AJ 94-5)

Like everyone else, [the Chhokling Rimpoche] spoke of masters, and the need of finding one, and how one finds one — of being drawn to him supernaturally, sometimes with instant recognition.

(AJ 97)

The purpose of words is to convey ideas. When the ideas are grasped, the words are forgotten.

Where can I find a man who has forgotten words? He is the one I would like to talk to.

(xxvi. II. WCZ 154)

One cannot understand Buddhism until one meets it in this existential manner, in a person in whom it is alive. Then there is no longer a problem of understanding doctrines ... but only a question of appreciating a value which is self-evident.

(ZBA 63)

A master is ... a child of the ancient Fathers, who bears their tradition with him and transmits it to future generations.... He is one who knows the unknown not by intellectual penetration, or by a science that wrests for itself the secrets of heaven, but by the wisdom of "littleness" and silence which knows how to receive in a secret a word that cannot be uttered except in an enigma.

(MZM 72–3)

16

"For he who knows does not speak,
He who speaks does not know"
And "The Wise Man gives instruction
Without the use of speech."

(WCZ 120)

It becomes overwhelmingly important for us *to become
detached from our everyday conception of ourselves as po-
tential subjects for special and unique experiences, or as
candidates for realization, attainment and fulfillment....* A
spiritual guide worth his salt will conduct a ruthless cam-
paign against all forms of delusion arising out of spiritual
ambition and self-complacency which aim to establish
the ego in spiritual glory.

(ZBA 76–7, italics Merton's)

Milarepa, angry, guilty of revenge, murder and black arts,
was purified by his master Marpa the translator who several times made him build a house many stones high and
then tear it down again. After which he was "no longer
the slave of his own psyche but its lord."

(AJ 84)

In order to become a "lamp for oneself," one must first
completely die to one's empirical "I," and to do this,
one must submit completely to another who is himself
enlightened and who knows exactly how to bring one
through the perilous ways of transformation and enlightenment. But in no case must one become attached to the
methods, the teaching the "system" ... of this master.

(MZM 225)

All creatures have gifts of their own.
The white horned owl can catch fleas at midnight

And distinguish the tip of a hair,
But in bright day it stares, helpless,
And cannot even see a mountian
All things have varying capacities.   (*WCZ* 88)

Water is for fish
And air for men.
Natures differ, and needs with them.

Hence the wise men of old
Did not lay down
One measure for all.   (xviii.5. *WCZ* 104)

How should you treat a bird?
As yourself
Or as a bird?   (*WCZ* 103)

"You must be your own lamps, be your own refuges. Take
refuge in nothing outside yourselves. Hold firm to the
truth as a lamp and a refuge, and do not look for a refuge
in anything besides yourselves."

        (*MZM* 218, quoting the Buddha)

I ask nobody to follow me. Everyone should follow his
own inner voice.   (II-205, *GNV* 48)

Don't listen to friends when the Friend inside you says
"Do this!"   (I-182, *GNV* 67)

Follow the ways of no man, not even your own. The way that is most yours is no way. For where are you? Unborn! Your way therefore is unborn. Yet you travel. You do not become unborn by stopping a journey you have begun: and you cannot be nowhere by issuing a decree: "I am now nowhere!"

(CP 421)

God alone knows the mind of a person; and the duty of a man of God is to act as he is directed by his inner voice. I claim that I act accordingly.

(II-204, GNV 48)

THE SELF

Buddhism and Christian monasticism start from the problem inside man himself. Instead of dealing with the external structures of society, they start with man's own consciousness. Both Christianity and Buddhism agree that the root of man's problems is that his consciousness is all fouled up and he does not apprehend reality as it fully and really is.... This is called by Buddhism avidya, or ignorance.

(*AJ* 332)

Buddha neither said "there is a self" or "there is not a self."... Buddha replied by silence because he considered the *condition of the questioner* and the effect of a dogmatic reply on him.

(*AJ* 104, italics Merton's)

We are plagued today with the heritage of that Cartesian self-awareness, which assumed that the empirical ego is the starting point of an infallible intellectual progress to truth and spirit.

(*MZM* 26)

The empirical ego is in fact the source and center of every illusion.

(MZM 224)

Buddha taught that all evil is rooted in the "ignorance" which makes us take our individual ego as our true self.... The root of personality is to be sought in the "true Self" which is manifested in the basic unification of consciousness in which subject and object are one. Hence the highest good is "the self's fusion with the highest reality." Human personality is regarded as the force which effects this fusion.

(ZBA 69)

Personalism and individualism must not be confused. Personalism gives priority to the *person* and not the individual self. To give priority to the person means respecting the unique and inalienable value of the *other* person, as well as one's own, for a respect that is centered only on one's individual self to the exclusion of others proves itself to be fraudulent.

(WCZ 17, italics Merton's)

At every turn, we get back to the big question, which is the question of the person as void and not as individual or empirical ego.... What is most ourselves is what is least ourselves.... It is the void that is our personality, and not our individuality that seems to be concrete and defined and present etc. It is what is seemingly not present, the void, that is really I. And the "I" that seems to be I is really a void. But the West is so used to identifying the person with the individual and the deeper self with the empirical self...that the basic truth is never seen. It is the Not-I that is most of all the I in each one of us.   (*HGL* 627)

Suffering, as both Christianity and Buddhism see, each in its own way, is part of our very ego-identity and empirical existence, and the only thing to do about it is to plunge right into the middle of contradiction and confusion in order to be transformed by what Zen calls the "Great Death" and Christianity calls "dying and rising with Christ."   (*ZBA* 51)

The basic aim of Buddhism, says Nhất Hạnh, arises out of human experience itself—the experience of suffering.... The problem of suffering is insoluble as long as men are prevented by their collective and individual illusions from getting directly to grips with suffering in its very root within themselves.   (*MZM* 286)

It is in surrendering a false and illusory liberty on the superficial level that man unites himself with the inner ground of reality and freedom in himself which is the will of God, of Krishna, of Providence, of Tao.   (*AJ* 353)

The self is not its own center and does not orbit around itself; it is centered on God, the one center of all, which is "everywhere and nowhere," in whom all are encountered, from whom all proceed. Thus from the very start this consciousness is disposed to encounter "the other" with whom it is already united anyway "in God."

The metaphysical intuition of Being is an intuition of a *ground of openness*, indeed of a kind of ontological openness and an infinite generosity which communicates itself to everything that is. "The good is diffusive of itself," or "God is love." Openness is not something to be acquired, but a radical gift that has been lost and must be recovered.

(*ZBA* 24–5, italics Merton's)

The "mind of Christ" as described by St. Paul in Philippians 2 may be theologically worlds apart from the "mind of Buddha."... But the utter "self-emptying" of Christ—and the self-emptying which makes the disciple one with Christ in *His* kenosis—can be understood ... in a very Zen-like sense as far as psychology and experience are concerned.

(*ZBA* 8, italics Merton's)

We accept our emptying because we realize that our very emptiness is fulfillment and plentitude. In our emptiness the One Word is clearly spoken.

(*IEW* 97)

If you can empty your own boat
Crossing the river of the world,
No one will oppose you,
No one will seek to harm you.

(xx.2, *WCZ* 114)

Once we live in awareness of the cosmic dance and move in time with the Dancer, our life attains its true dimension.... To live without this illuminated consciousness is to live as a beast of burden, carrying one's life with tragic seriousness as a huge, incomprehensible weight.... The weight of the burden is the seriousness with which one takes one's own individual and separate self. To live with the true consciousness of life centered in Another is to lose one's self-important seriousness and thus to live life as "play" in union with a Cosmic Player. (*AJ* 350)

To live selflessly is to live in joy, realizing by experience that life itself is love and gift. To be a lover and a giver is to be a channel through which the Supreme Giver manifests His love in the world. (*AJ* 350)

At the very center of man's being is an intimate, dynamic principle of reality. It is not merely a static concept or essence, but a "nature" constantly seeking to express its reality in right action. In this way, the hidden reality of heaven communicates itself to the man who is in harmony with it by his actions. *Reality* is the goal, and reality in act is the "axis" or "pivot" of man's being. The "superior man" is one who finds this axis in himself and lives always centered upon it. (*MZM* 59, italics Merton's)

The spirit of non-violence sprang from *an inner realization of spiritual unity in himself.* The whole Gandhian concept of non-violent action and *satyagraha* is ... *the fruit of inner unity already achieved.* (*GNV* 10, italics Merton's)

The foundation of Confucian system is first of all the *human person* and then his relations with other persons in society. (*MZM* 51, italics Merton's)

The order of society depends on awareness, right action, and self-discipline in all its members from the ruler to the least of common men. The peace and order of the community depend on the discipline of awareness by which each member recognizes what is to be done by him, or what properly accords with his identity and function in the community. *(MZM 61)*

Our evils are common and the solution of them can only be common. But we are not ready to undertake this common task because we are not ourselves. Consequently the first duty of every man is to return to his own "right mind" in order that society may be sane. *(GNV 25)*

"We are at war with ourselves," said Coomaraswamy, "and therefore at war with one another. Western man is unbalanced, and the question, Can he recover himself? is a very real one." *(GNV 6)*

There can be no peace on earth without the kind of inner change that brings man back to his "right mind." *(GNV 31)*

"Myself." No-self. The self is merely a locus in which the dance of the universe is aware of itself as complete from beginning to end—and returning to the void. Gladly. Praising, giving thanks, with all beings. Christ light—spirit—grace—gift. (Bodhicitta) *(AJ 68)*

ZEN

By Zen we mean precisely the quest for direct and pure experience on a metaphysical level, liberated from verbal formulas and linguistic preconceptions.　(*ZBA* 44)

Zen implies a breakthrough, an explosive liberation from one-dimensional conformism, a recovery of unity which is not the suppression of opposites but a simplicity beyond opposites.　(*ZBA* 140)

What Zen communicates is an awareness that is potentially already there but is not conscious of itself. Zen is then not Kerygma but realization, not revelation but consciousness, not news from the Father who sends His Son into the world, but awareness of the ontological ground of our own being here and now, right in the midst of the world.　(*ZBA* 47)

Any attempt to handle Zen in theological language is bound to miss the point.　(*ZBA* 139)

We must admit it is perfectly logical to admit, with the Zen Masters, that "Zen teaches nothing."   (*ZBA* 47)

Zen is outside all particular structures and distinct forms ... it is neither opposed to them nor not-opposed to them. It neither denies them nor affirms them, loves them nor hates them, rejects them nor desires them. Zen is consciousness unstructured by particular form or particular system, a trans-cultural, trans-religious, trans-formed consciousness.   (*ZBA* 4)

Zen cannot be grasped as long as one remains passively conformed to *any* cultural or social imperatives, whether ideological, sociological, or what have you.
    (*ZBA* 140, italics Merton's)

[Zen] is nondoctrinal, concrete, direct, existential, and seeks above all to come to grips with life itself, not with ideas about life, still less with party platforms in politics, religion, science, or anything else.   (*ZBA* 32)

The Zen experience is a direct grasp of the *unity* of the invisible and the visible, the noumenal and the phenomenal ... an experiential realization that any such division is bound to be pure imagination.   (*ZBA* 37, italics Merton's)

The first and most elementary fact about Zen is its abhorrence of this dualistic division between matter and spirit.   (*MZM* 13)

Zen is a way of insight rather than a way of "salvation."

(*MZM* 247)

"The whole system of Zen ... may thus be said to be nothing but a series of attempts to set us free from all forms of bondage." (*MZM* 222, quoting D. T. Suzuki)

EMPTINESS / *SUNYATA*

From emptiness comes the unconditioned.
From this, the conditioned, the individual things.
So from the sage's emptiness, stillness arises:
From stillness, action. From action, attainment.
From their stillness comes their non-action, which is also
    action
And is, therefore, their attainment.
For stillness is joy. Joy is free from care
Fruitful in long years.
Joy does all things without concern:
From emptiness, stillness, tranquility, tastelessness,
Silence, and non-action
Are the root of all things.   (xiii.I., *WCZ* 81)

The perfect act is empty. Who can see it? He who forgets
form. Out of the formed, the unformed, the empty act
proceeds with its own form. Perfect form is momentary.
Its perfection vanishes at once. Perfection and emptiness
work together for they are the same: the coincidence of
momentary form and eternal nothingness. Form: the

flash of nothingness. Forget form, and it suddenly appears, ringed and reverberating with its own light, which is nothing. Well, then: stop seeking. Let it all happen. Let it come and go. What? Everything: i.e., nothing.

(CP 421)

ENLIGHTENMENT / *SATORI*

Song for Nobody

A yellow flower
(Light and spirit)
Sings by itself
For nobody.

A golden spirit
(Light and emptiness)
Sings without a word
By itself.

Let no one touch this gentle sun
In whose dark eye
Someone is awake.

(No light, no gold, no name, no color
And no thought:
O, wide awake!)

A golden heaven
Sings by itself
A song to nobody.   (CP 337–38)

From the moment a man is immersed in confusion
and carried away by the passions and eccentricities of a
bewildered and not always upright society, he has little
hope of finding himself merely by shutting his eyes and
following the *Tao*. The *Tao* may be within him, but he
is completely out of touch with it, just as he is out of
touch with his own inmost self. Recovery of the *Tao* is
impossible without a complete transformation, a change
of heart, which Christianity would call *metanoia*. Zen ...
envisaged this problem, and studied at how to arrive at
satori, or the explosive rediscovery of the hidden and lost
reality within us.   (MZM 50)

Buddhism does not seek primarily to understand or to
"believe in" the enlightenment of Buddha as the solution
to all human problems, but seeks an existential and empirical participation in that enlightenment experience.
                                               (ZBA 36)

If you are attached to worldly things you are not a
     religious man.
If you are attached to appearances you cannot meditate.
If you are attached to your own soul you cannot have
     bodhicitta.
If you are attached to doctrines you cannot reach the
     highest attainment.   (AJ 120–21)

When we are empty we become capable of fullness (which has never been absent from us).   (*ZBA* 137)

In Buddhism … the highest development of consciousness is that by which the individual ego is completely emptied and becomes identified with the enlightened Buddha, or rather finds itself to be in reality the enlightened Buddha mind. Nirvana is not the consciousness of an ego that is aware of itself as having crossed over to "the other shore" … but the Absolute Ground–Consciousness of the Void, in which there are no shores. Thus the Buddhist enters into the self-emptying and enlightenment of Buddha as the Christian enters into the self-emptying (crucifixion) and glorification (resurrection and ascension) of Christ. The chief difference between the two is that the former is existential and ontological, the latter is theological and personal. But "person" here must be distinguished from "the individual empirical ego."   (*ZBA* 76)

Zen is not *our* awareness, but Being's awareness of itself in us.   (*MZM* 17, italics Merton's)

Personally I do not think satori is impossible for a Christian any more than it is for a Buddhist. In either case, one goes in a certain sense beyond all categories, religious or otherwise.   (*HGL* 443)

The Zen insight is the awareness of full spiritual reality, and therefore the realization of the emptiness of all limited or particularized realities.   (*MZM* 17)

As the Buddhists say, *Nirvana* is found in the midst of the world around us, and truth is not *somewhere else.* To be here and now where we are in our "suchness" is to be in *Nirvana.*   (*ZBA* 87, italics Merton's)

Nirvana is beyond experience. Yet it is also the "highest experience" if we see it as a liberation from merely psychological limitations. The words "experience of love" must not be understood in terms of emotional fulfillment ... but of full realization, total awakening—a complete realization of love not merely as the emotion of a feeling subject but as the wide openness of Being itself, the realization that Pure Being is Infinite Giving, or that Absolute Emptiness is Absolute Compassion.

(*ZBA* 86, italics Merton's)

Nirvana: perfect awareness and perfect compassion. *Nirvana* is the wisdom of perfect love grounded in itself and shining through everything, meeting with no opposition.

(*ZBA* 84, italics Merton's)

If you once penetrate by detachment and purity of heart to the inner secret of the ground of your ordinary experience, you attain to a liberty that nobody can touch.

(*AJ* 342)

Once we live in awareness of the cosmic dance and move in time with the Dancer, our life attains its true dimension.

(*AJ* 350)

ON PRACTICE /
"SKILLFUL MEANS"

"SKILLFUL MEANS": GENERAL

The future will depend on what we do in the present.

(II-259, GNV 92)

The great contemplative traditions of East and West, while differing sometimes quite radically in their formulation of their aims and in their understanding of their methods, agree in thinking that by spiritual disciplines a man can radically change his life and attain to a deeper meaning, a more perfect integration, a more complete fulfillment, a more total liberty of spirit than are possible in the routines of a purely active existence centered on money-making. There is more to human life than just "getting somewhere" in war, politics, business.

(MZM viii)

Chuang Tzu himself would be the first to say that you cannot tell people to do whatever they want when they don't even know what they want in the first place!

(WCZ 16)

Once a man has sent his foot on this way, there is no excuse for abandoning it, for to be actually on the way is to recognize without doubt or hesitation that only the way is fully real and that everything else is deception, except in so far as it may in some secret and hidden manner be connected with "the way."   (*IEW* 67)

Christianity is first of all a way of life, rather than a way of thought.   (*IEW* 77)

I think the dialogue between Christianity and Buddhism will be most fruitful on the plane not of abstract metaphysical systems but on the plane of what I would call metaphysical experience—that is to say, the basic intuition of being the direct grasp of the ground of reality, which is essential to a true and lived metaphysics. I repeat that I am not concerned with purely abstract metaphysical systems. The basic metaphysical intuition is close to the kind of religious intuition which opens out into mysticism. On this level I think we come very close to what Buddhism is saying. On this level Zen seems to me something very close to home, very alive, very helpful, indeed necessary. In Christian metaphysical-and-mystical experience there is something very close to Zen.   (*WF* 332)

Even where there are irreconcilable differences in doctrine and in formulated belief, there may still be great similarities and analogies in the realm of religious experience.   (*AJ* 312)

The method should suit one's character. After correct practice one feels "cool, bright, and calm." *(AJ 15)*

Both Buddhism and Christianity are alike in making use of ordinary everyday human existence as material for a radical transformation of consciousness. *(ZBA 51)*

At the end of Zen training, when one has become "absolutely naked," one finds himself to be the ordinary "Tom, Dick or Harry" that he has been all along. *(ZBA 118)*

Zen saying: before I grasped Zen, the mountains were nothing but mountains and the rivers nothing but rivers. When I got into Zen, the mountains were no longer mountains and the rivers no longer rivers. But when I understood Zen, the mountains were only mountains and the rivers only rivers. *(ZBA 140)*

Where the fountains of passion
Lie deep
The heavenly springs
Are soon dry. *(WCZ 60)*

The true tranquility sought by the "man of Tao" is *Ying ning*, tranquility in the action of non-action . . . a tranquility which transcends the division between activity and contemplation by entering into union with the nameless and invisible Tao. *(WCZ 26)*

The *Bhagavad-Gita* can be seen as the great treatise on the "Active Life." But it is essentially something more, for it tends to fuse worship, action, and contemplation in a fulfillment of daily duty which transcends all three by virtue of a higher consciousness: a consciousness of acting passively, of being an obedient instrument of a transcendent will. (*AJ* 348)

"To know when to stop
To know when you can get no further
By your own action,
This is the right beginning!" (xxiii.3–7, *WCZ* 133)

For each of us there is a point of nowhereness in the middle of movement, a point of nothingness in the midst of being: the incomparable point, not to be discovered by insight. If you seek it you do not find it. If you stop seeking, it is there. But you must not turn to it. Once you become aware of yourself as seeker, you are lost. But if you are content to be lost you will be found without knowing it, precisely because you are lost, for you are, at last, nowhere. (*CP* 452)

CONTEMPLATIVE LIFE

It is absolutely essential to introduce into our study of the humanities a dimension of *wisdom* oriented to contemplation as well as to wise action. For this, it is no longer sufficient merely to go back over the Christian and European cultural traditions. The horizons of the world are no longer confined to Europe and America. We have to gain new perspectives, and on this our spiritual and even our physical survival may depend. (*MZM* 80, italics Merton's)

The contemplative life must provide an area, a space of liberty, of silence, in which possibilities are allowed to surface and new choices—beyond routine choices—become manifest. It should create a new experience of time, not as stopgap, stillness, but as "temps vierge"—not a blank to be filled or an untouched space to be conquered and violated, but a space which can enjoy its own potentialities and hopes—and its own presence to itself. One's *own* time. But not dominated by one's own ego and its demands. Hence open to others—*compassionate* time, rooted in the sense of common illusion and criticism of it.

(*AJ* 117, italics Merton's)

Chuang Tzu held that only when one was in contact with the mysterious Tao which is beyond all existent things, which cannot be conveyed either by words or by silence, and which is apprehended only in a state which is neither speech nor silence (xxv.II.) could one really understand how to live. (*WCZ* 21)

Chuang Tzu is not concerned with words and formulas about reality, but with the direct existential grasp of reality in itself. (*WCZ* 11)

The goal of the contemplative is, on its lowest level, the recognition of this splendor of being and unity — a splendor in which he is one with all that is. (*IEW* 69)

One cannot call Chuang Tzu a "contemplative" in the sense of one who adopts a systematic program of spiritual self-purification in order to attain certain definite spiritual experiences, or even merely to "cultivate the interior life." Chuang Tzu would condemn this just as roundly as the "cultivation" of anything else on an artificial basis. All deliberate, systematic, and reflexive "self cultivation" ... cuts one off from the mysterious but indispensable contact with Tao, the hidden "Mother" of all life and truth. (*WCZ* 26)

The way of Tao is to begin with the simple good with which one is endowed by the very fact of existence. (*WCZ* 23)

The inner journey is the interpolation of the meanings
and signs of our outer pilgrimage.   (*MZM* 92)

Every man knows how useful it is to be useful.

No one seems to know
How useful it is to be useless.   (iv.9, *WCZ* 59)

SOLITUDE

The man of spirit ... hates to see people gather around him. He avoids the crowd. For where there are many men, there are also many opinions and little agreement. There is nothing to be gained from the support of a lot of half-wits who are doomed to end up in a fight with each other. (*WCZ* 149)

The effect of life in society is to complicate and confuse our existence, making us forget who we really are by causing us to become obsessed with what we are not.
(*WCZ* 27)

The "man of Tao" will prefer obscurity and solitude.
(*WCZ* 25)

Only in silence and solitude, in the quiet of worship, the reverent peace of prayer, the adoration in which the entire ego-self silences and abases itself in the presence of the Invisible God, only in these "activities" which are

"non-actions" does the spirit truly wake from the dream
of a multifarious and confused existence.   (*IEW* 121)

Song: If You Seek …

If you seek a heavenly light
I, Solitude, am your professor!

I go before you into emptiness,
Raise strange suns for your new mornings,
Opening the windows
Of your innermost apartment.

When I, loneliness, give my special signal
Follow my silence, follow where I beckon!
Fear not, little beast, little spirit
(Thou word and animal)
I, Solitude, am angel
And have prayed in your name.

Look at the empty, wealthy night
The pilgrim moon!
I am the appointed hour,
The "now" that cuts
Time like a blade.

I am the unexpected flash
Beyond "yes," beyond "no,"
The forerunner of the Word of God.

Follow my ways and I will lead you
To golden-haired suns,
Logos and music, blameless joys,
Innocent of questions
And beyond answers:

For I, Solitude, am thine own self:
I, Nothingness, am thy All.
I, Silence, am thy Amen! (*CP* 340–41)

Contrary to what has been thought in recent centuries in the West, the spiritual or interior life is not an exclusively private affair.... The spiritual life of one person is simply the life of all manifesting itself in him. (*GNV* 11)

A solitary is not absent from the rest of men, and a solitude that merely excluded other men would be pure illusion. Yet a solitary prefers the silence and solitude of the woods, and he is most awake, most true to his calling. When he is with no one. Nevertheless he can share with others what he considers most precious: the climate of emptiness in which he lives. (*IEW* 122)

The true unity of the solitary life is the one in which there is no possible division. The true solitary does not seek himself, but loses himself. He forgets that there is number, in order to become all. (*IEW* 91)

"True love requires contact with the truth, and the truth must be found in solitude. The ability to bear solitude, and to spend long stretches of time alone by oneself in quiet meditation, is therefore one of the more elementary qualifications for those who aspire towards selfless love."

(AJ 157, quoting Conze)

Where is silence? Where is solitude? Where is Love? Ultimately, these cannot be found anywhere except in the ground of our own being. There, in the silent depths, there is no more distinction between the I and the Not-I. There is perfect peace because we are grounded in infinite creative and redemptive Love.

(IEW 94–5)

FASTING

It is quite possible for Zen to be adapted and used to clear the air of ascetic irrelevancies and help us to regain a healthy natural balance in our understanding of the spiritual life.   (*ZBA* 58)

Fasting remained primarily an act of worship and an act of witness to universal truth. It formed part of the Hindu *dharma* and therefore of India's witness to the religious truths implicit in the very structure of cosmic reality.

(*GNV* 14)

Fasting cannot be undertaken mechanically. It is a powerful thing but a dangerous thing if handled amateurishly. It requires complete self-purification much more than is required in facing death with retaliation in mind.

(II-165, *GNV* 89)

There is not room for imitation in fasts. He who has no inner strength should not dream of it, and never with attachment to success. But if a *satyagrahi* once undertakes a fast from conviction, he must stick to his resolve whether there is a change of his action bearing fruit or not.... He who fasts in expectation of fruit generally fails.

(II-48, *GNV* 87)

"Tell me," said Yen Hui, "what is fasting of the heart?"

Confucius replied: "The goal of fasting is inner unity.... Fasting of the heart empties the faculties, frees you from limitation and from preoccupation. Fasting of the heart begets unity and freedom." (*WCZ* 52–3)

Look at this window: it is nothing but a hole in the wall, but because of it the whole room is full of light. So when the faculties are empty, the heart is full of light. Being full of light it becomes an influence by which others are secretly transformed. (iv.I, *WCZ* 53)

POSSESSIONS

A society that lives by organized greed or by systematic terrorism and oppression ... will always tend to be violent because it is in a state of persistent disorder and moral confusion.   (*GNV* 15)

The life of riches, ambition, pleasure, is in reality an intolerable servitude in which one "lives for what is always out of reach," thirsting "for survival in the future" and "incapable of living in the present."   (*WCZ* 22)

It is those who acquire inordinate possessions for themselves and defend them against others, who make it necessary for the others to steal in order to make a living.
                                                        (*ZBA* 123)

... what the world calls good business is only a way
To gather up the loot, pack it, make it secure
In one convenient load for the more enterprising thieves.
Who is there, among those called smart,

Who does not spend his time amassing loot
For a bigger robber than himself.   (WCZ 67)

Buddhism considers that a fundamental geocentricism,
"providing for the self" (with possible economic impli-
cations in a more modern context) leads to dogmatism
about the self—either that it is eternal or that it does
not exist at all. A truly critical attitude implies a certain
freedom from predetermination by economic and sociological factors. The notion of "I" implies a notion of
"mine." I am "my property"—I am constituted by what
separates me from "not I"—i.e., by what is mine "and not
anybody's else."   (AJ 105)

He who is controlled by objects
Loses possession of his inner self:
If he no longer values himself,
How can he value others?   (WCZ 137)

"There is no limit whatsoever to the measure of sacrifice
that one may make in order to realize this *oneness with all
life,* but certainly the immensity of the ideal sets a limit
to your wants. That, you will see, is the antithesis of the
position of the modern civilization which says 'Increase
your wants.'... Hinduism rules out indulgence and mul-
tiplication of wants, as these hamper one's growth to the
ultimate identity with the Universal Self."

(GNV 15, quoting Gandhi, italics
and punctuation as in original)

PRAYERS / PRAYING

Our real journey in life is interior; it is a matter of growth, deepening, and of an ever greater surrender to the creative action of love and grace in our hearts. Never was it more necessary for us to respond to that action. I pray that we may all do so. (*AJ* 296)

[*Untitled*]

Five breaths pray in me: sun moon
Rain wind and fire
Five seated Buddhas reign in the breaths
Five illusions
One universe:
The white breath, yellow breath,
Green breath, blue breath,
Red fire breath, Amitabha
Knowledge and Desire
And the quiescence
Of Knowledge and Desire. (*CP* 785)

Prayer flags flutter among the trees. Rock mandalas are along all the pathways. OM MANI PADME HUM ("Hail to the jewel in the lotus") is carved on every boulder. It is moving to see so many Tibetans going about silently praying—almost all of them are constantly carrying rosaries.   (AJ 93)

Yesterday as I came down the path from the mountain I heard a strange humming behind me. A Tibetan came by quietly droning a monotonous sound, a prolonged "om." It was something that harmonized with the mountain—an ancient syllable he had found long ago in the rocks—or perhaps it had been born with him.   (AJ 79)

Prayer is not an old woman's idle amusement. Properly understood and applied, it is the most potent instrument of action.   (II-77, GNV 87)

My greatest weapon is mute prayer.   (I-251, GNV 59)

From "Freedom as Experience"

And so, some days in prayer Your Love,
Prisoning us in darkness from the values of Your universe,
Delivers us from measure and from time,
Melts all the barriers that stop our passage to eternity
And solves the hours our chains.

And then, as fires like jewels germinate
Deep in the stone heart of a Kaffir mountain,

So now our gravity, our new-created deep desire
Burns in our life's mind like an undiscovered diamond.

Locked in that strength we stay and stay
And cannot go away
For You have given us our liberty.

Imprisoned in the fortunes of Your adamant
We can no longer move, for we are free. (*CP* 187)

Oh God, we are one with You. You have made us one
with You. You have taught us that if we are open to one
another, You dwell in us. Help us to preserve this openness.... Help us to realize that there can be no understanding where there is mutual rejection. Oh God, in
accepting one another wholeheartedly, fully, completely,
we accept You, and we thank You, and we adore You, and
we love You with our whole being, because our being is
in Your being, our spirit is rooted in Your spirit. Fill us
then with love, and let us be bound together with love
... united in this one spirit which makes You present in
the world, and which makes You witness to the ultimate
reality that is love. Love has overcome. Love is victori-
ous. Amen. (*AJ* 318–19)

MEDITATION

Honestly I do not think it matters a bit whether one can
sit cross-legged or not. *(HGL 442)*

[The Dalai Lama] demonstrated the sitting position for
meditation which he said was essential. In the Tibetan
meditation posture the right hand (discipline) is above
the left (wisdom). In Zen it is the other way round. Then
we go to "concentrating on the mind." Other objects of
concentration may be an object, an image, a name. But
how does one concentrate on the mind itself? *(AJ 112–13)*

Does Buddhist meditation deny the body entirely and
seek to pass over into a realm of purely spiritual abstrac-
tion? Quite the contrary. The body plays a most important part in Buddhist meditation, in fact in no other
meditation discipline is the body so important. Instead
of eliminating, or trying to eliminate, all body-conscious-
ness, Buddhist meditation is keenly aware of the body.
In order to master the mind, Buddhist meditation seeks
first of all to master the body. *(ZBA 95)*

When the delights become a religion, how can you control them?

(WCZ 71)

"First gain control of the body
And all its organs. Then
Control the mind. Attain
One-pointedness. Then
The harmony of heaven
Will come down and dwell in you.
You will be radiant with Life.
You will rest in Tao."

(WCZ 121)

"The true conqueror is he
Who is not conquered
By the multitude of the small.
The mind is this conqueror—
But only the mind
Of the wise man."

(xvii.4-5-8, WCZ 90)

"My body is chaos
But my mind is in order"

(WCZ 62)

"Hold your being secure and quiet,
Keep your life collected in its own center.
Do not allow your thoughts
To be disturbed."

(WCZ 128)

Buddhist "mindfulness" or awareness, which in its most
elementary form consists in that "bare attention" which
simply *sees* what is right there and does not add any com-

ment, any interpretation, any judgment, any conclusion. It just *sees*. Learning to see in this manner is the basic and fundamental exercise of Buddhist meditation.

(ZBA 53, italics Merton's)

Zen uses language against itself to blast out … preconceptions and to destroy the specious "reality" in our minds so that we can *see directly*. Zen is saying, as Wittgenstein said, "Don't think. Look!"

(ZBA 49, italics Merton's)

Buddhist meditation, but above all that of Zen, seeks not to *explain* but to *pay attention*, to *become aware*, to *be mindful*, in other words to develop a certain *kind of consciousness that is above and beyond deception* by verbal formulas—or by emotional excitement.

(ZBA 38, italics Merton's)

The Son Who, in us, loves the Father, in the Spirit, is translated thus by Suzuki into Zen terms: "one mirror reflecting another with no shadow between them." Suzuki also frequently quotes a sentence of Eckhart's: "the eye wherein I see God is the same eye wherein God sees me" … as an exact expression of what Zen means by *Prajna*.

(ZBA 57, italics Merton's)

"To exercise no-thought
And follow no-way of meditation
Is the first step toward understanding Tao.
To dwell nowhere

And rest in nothing
Is the first step toward resting in Tao.
To start from nowhere
And follow no road
Is the first step toward attaining Tao." (*WCZ* 119)

NON-VIOLENCE / *AHIMSA*

AHIMSA (non-violence) is for Gandhi the basic law of
our being. That is why it can be used as the most effective
principle for social action, since it is in deep accord with
the truth of man's nature and corresponds to his innate
desire for peace, justice, order, freedom, and personal
dignity. (*GNV* 35)

Violence is essentially wordless, and it can begin only
where thought and rational communication have broken
down. Any society which is geared for violent action is by
that very fact systematically unreasonable and inarticulate.
(*GNV* 13)

Satyagraha is meaningless if it is not based on the awareness of profound inner contradiction in all societies
based on force. (*GNV* 15–6)

Buddhist "mindfulness," far from being contemptuous of
life, is extremely solicitious for all life. (*ZBA* 93)

A religion which forbids the taking of *any* life without absolute necessity is hardly "life denying."

(ZBA 15–16, italics Merton's)

In order to be holy one must become free from the tyranny of the demands of sin, of lust, of anger, of pride, ambition, injustice, and the spirit of violence.   (*IEW* 78)

Non-cooperation with evil is a sacred duty.

(I-358, GNV 70)

"If you can avoid evil by suffering it yourself, do so."

(GNV 23, quoting Erasmus)

The man in whom Tao
Acts without impediment
Harms no other being
By his actions
Yet he does not know himself
To be "kind," to be "gentle."   (*WCZ* 91)

The only way truly to "overcome" an enemy is to help him become other than an enemy.   (*GNV* 24)

The oppressed must be able to be free within himself, so that he may begin to gain strength to pity his oppressor. Without that capacity for pity, neither of them will be able to recognize the truth of their situation: a common relationship in a common complex of sins.   (*GNV* 23)

To punish and destroy the oppressor is merely to initiate a new cycle of violence and oppression. The only real liberation is that which *liberates both the oppressor and the oppressed.*"

(*GNV* 22, italics Merton's)

Where there is *ahimsa* there is Truth and Truth is God. How He manifests Himself I cannot say. All I know is that He is all pervading and where He is all is well.

(II-151, *GNV* 47)

Paper Cranes

(The Hibakusha come to Gethsemani)

How can we tell a paper bird
Is stronger than a hawk
When it has no metal for talons?
It needs no power to kill
Because it is not hungry.

Wilder and wiser than eagles
It ranges round the world
Without enemies
And free of cravings.

The child's hand
Folding these wings
Wins no wars and ends them all.

Thoughts of a child's heart
Without care, without weapons!
So the child's eye
Gives life to what it loves
Kind as the innocent sun
And lovelier than all dragons!   (CP 740)

COMPASSION

Only the admission of defect and fallibility in oneself makes it possible for one to become merciful to others.

(GNV 20)

The rimpoches all advise against absolute solitude and stress "compassion." They seem to agree that being in solitude much of the year and coming "out" for a while would be a good solution.

(AJ 103)

The Khempo of Namgyal [said that] the real ground of his Gelugpa study and practice was the knowledge of suffering, and that only when a person was fully convinced of the immensity of suffering and its complete universality and saw the need of deliverance from it, and sought deliverance for *all* beings, could he begin to understand sunyata.

(AJ, 94, italics Merton's)

The Bodhisattva elects to remain in [the phenomenal world] and finds in it his *Nirvana*, by reason ... of the compassionate love which identifies all the sufferers in

the round of birth and death with the Buddha, whose
enlightenment they potentially share.   (ZBA 38)

Jen is sometimes translated "human heartedness."
                                               (WCZ 18)

Jen is the compassion that enables one to identify with
the joys and troubles of others.   (WCZ 157)

Compassion is proportionate to detachment; otherwise we use others for our own ends under the pretext
of "love." Actually, we are dominated by illusion. Love
that perpetuates the illusion does no good to others or
to ourselves. Ultimately the illusion has to be destroyed
by prajna, which is also one with perfect compassion
(karuna).   (AJ 157–58)

The cornerstone of all Gandhi's life, action, and thought
was the respect for the sacredness of life and the conviction that "love is the law of our being."   (GNV 17)

The whole idea of compassion, which is central to Mahayana Buddhism, is based on a keen awareness of the
interdependence of all these living beings, which are all
part of one another and all involved in one another.
                                               (AJ 341–42)

Oh God, we are one with You. You have made us one
with You. You have taught us that if we are open to one
another, You dwell in us...."   (AJ 318)

The disciple, blindfolded, is led to the east gate of the prepared mandala. Blindfolded, he casts a flower on the mandala. The flower will find his way for him into the palace. Follow your flower!   (AJ 86)

GLOSSARY

EDITOR'S NOTE: Most of these brief definitions of key, but possibly unfamiliar, terms are abstracted from longer entries in the glossary of *The Asian Journal of Thomas Merton* (363–418). References not otherwise designated are to page numbers in that volume. Uncited entries are the editor's.

Ahimsa: Non-violence.

Amitabha: Buddha of the Great Vehicle who vowed to create a pure land ... and to save all having faith in his vows. Also known, especially in Japan, as Amida.   (364)

Ananda: A favorite disciple of the Buddha.   (364)

Avidya: The Sanskrit term for ignorance or nonawareness.   (368)

Bhagavad-Gita: Sanskrit, the discourse between Krishna and Arjuna that forms [probably the most famous] part of the Indian epic the *Mahabharata*. (*AJ* 368)

Bodhicitta: The thought of enlightenment. Human consciousness. The Buddha-mind, the Buddha-nature. (369)

Bodhisattva: One who having attained enlightenment (bodhi) is on his way to Buddhahood but postpones his goal to keep a vow to help all life attain salvation. (369)

Cartesian: Adjective describing the philosophy developed by Rene Decartes who wrote "I think, therefore, I am."

Dharma: The way, the law, righteousness, reality. The path which a man should follow in accordance with his nature and station in life. (371–72)

Dharmakaya: The cosmic body of the Buddha, the essence of all beings. (372)

Gelugpa: "Yellow Hats," one of the four principal sects of Tibetan Buddhism and the one to which the Dalai Lama belongs. (375)

Guru: A sage, teacher, or venerable holy person, particularly a spiritual guide; one who takes disciples for religious instruction.

Jen: Compassion or human heartedness. One of the four basic virtues of Confucian ethics, Jen is the compassion that enables one to identify with the joys and troubles of others. (*WCZ* 18 and 157)

Kanchenjunga: One of the most spectacular peaks of the Himalayas. (380)

Karuna: The Mahayana Buddhist term for compassion; a trait of bodhisattvas. (381)

Kenosis: A Greek word for "emptiness." St. Paul chooses the verb form to describe Jesus' self-giving in Philippians 2:7: "he emptied himself."

Kerygma: Greek word for "teaching" or "proclamation," specifically preaching for conversion.

Krishna: One of the most important gods in the Hindu pantheon, the eighth avatar (earthly incarnation) of the god Vishnu. (382)

Mahayana: From *mahat* great + *yana* vehicle … a branch of Buddhism made up of various syncretistic sects that are found chiefly in Tibet, Nepal, China, and Japan … and usually teach the bodhisattva ideal of compassion and universal salvation. (385)

Mara: The spirit or personification of evil; enemy of the Buddha. (386)

Milarepa: Tibet's greatest poet, considered a saint. (387)

Nirvana: The attainment of final enlightenment; freedom from rebirth. (389)

Prajna: Supreme knowledge or wisdom; spiritual awakening; wisdom which brings liberation. (393)

Satori: In Zen Buddhism, awakening, illumination, enlightenment. (401)

Satyagraha: Non-violent protest or resistence for social change taught by M. K. Gandhi.

Sunyata: Emptiness, the Void. (405)

Tao: The Way, the Absolute, the Ultimate Principle.
(*WCZ* 157)

ACKNOWLEDGMENTS

Thanks are due for permission to quote from the following copyrighted source: *Mystics and Zen Masters* by Thomas Merton. Copyright © 1967 by the Abbey of Gethsemani. Copyright renewed 1995 by Robert Giroux, James Laughlin, and Tommy O'Callaghan as trustees of the Merton Legacy Trust. Reprinted by permission of Farrar, Straus and Giroux, LLC.

Grateful acknowledgement is made to the editors and publishers of the following books in which material in this volume first appeared or from whom permission to reprint has been obtained: *The Hidden Ground of Love: The Letters of Thomas Merton on Religious Experience and Social Concerns*, ed. William H. Shannon (New York: Farrar, Straus and Giroux); *Introductions East and West*, ed. Robert E. Daggy (Greensboro: Unicorn Press); *Mystics and Zen Masters*, (New York: Farrar, Straus and Giroux — reprinted by permission of Farrar, Straus and Giroux); *Witness to Freedom: The Letters of Thomas Merton in Times of Crisis*, ed. William H. Shannon (New York: Farrar, Straus and Giroux).

Further acknowledgment is made to the editors and publishers of all other cited material by Thomas Merton.